the Master SPY Handbook

HELP OUR INTREPID HERO USE GADGETS, CODES & TOP-SECRET TACTICS TO SAVE THE WORLD FROM EVILDOERS

RAIN NEWCOMB

ILLUSTRATED BY **JASON CHIN**

LARK BOOKS

A Division of
Sterling Publishing Co., Inc.
New York

CREATIVE DIRECTOR
CELIA NARANJO

EDITOR
JOE RHATIGAN

TECHNICAL ILLUSTRATOR
ORRIN LUNDGREN

EDITORIAL ASSISTANCE
DELORES GOSNELL
AND
VERONIKA ALICE GUNTER

EDITORIAL INTERNS
KELLY J. JOHNSON
AND
METTA PRY

PROOFREADER
KAREN LEVY

Newcomb, Rain.
   The master spy handbook : help our intrepid hero use gadgets, codes & top-secret tactics to save the world from evildoers / by Rain Newcomb ;
illustrated by Jason Chin.— 1st ed.
      p. cm.
   Includes index.
   ISBN 1-57990-626-5 (hardcover)
   1. Espionage—Juvenile literature. 2. Handicraft—Juvenile literature.
   I. Title.
   UB270.5.N47 2005
   327.12—dc22

                                                2005009201

10 9 8 7 6 5 4 3 2 1

First Edition

Published by Lark Books, A Division of
Sterling Publishing Co., Inc.
387 Park Avenue South, New York, N.Y. 10016

Text © 2005, Lark Books
Illustrations © 2005, Jason Chin

Distributed in Canada by Sterling Publishing,
c/o Canadian Manda Group, 165 Dufferin Street
Toronto, Ontario, Canada M6K 3H6

Distributed in the U.K. by Guild of Master Craftsman
Publications Ltd., Castle Place, 166 High Street, Lewes,
East Sussex, England BN7 1XU
Tel: (+ 44) 1273 477374, Fax: (+ 44) 1273 478606,
e-mail: pubs@thegmcgroup.com,
Web: www.gmcpublications.com

Distributed in Australia by
Capricorn Link (Australia) Pty Ltd.,
P.O. Box 704, Windsor, NSW 2756 Australia

The written instructions, photographs, designs, patterns, and projects in this volume are intended for the personal use of the reader and may be reproduced for that purpose only. Any other use, especially commercial use, is forbidden under law without written permission of the copyright holder.

Every effort has been made to ensure that all the information in this book is accurate. However, due to differing conditions, tools, and individual skills, the publisher cannot be responsible for any injuries, losses, and other damages that may result from the use of the information in this book.

If you have questions or comments about this book, please contact:
Lark Books
67 Broadway
Asheville, NC 28801
(828) 253-0467

Manufactured in China

ISBN 1-57990-626-5

For information about custom editions, special sales, premium and corporate purchases, please contact Sterling Special Sales Department at 800-805-5489 or special-sales@sterlingpub.com.

CONTENTS

Dear Reader,

One hot summer day, as I was reclining in my hammock, I noticed something peculiar about one of the ice cubes in my lemonade. I fished it out with a spoon and cracked it open. This was the message I found inside the ice cube: "Help me write a book to show kids how to be master spies."

And that's how I "met" Agent O, the world's greatest spy. All summer long I received Agent O's personal spy notes and folders, each of which included tips for becoming a super spy, great spy gadgets to make, and disguise techniques that would fool your mother. I have collected more than 50 of these techniques and tips in this book.

But why would Agent O divulge this top-secret information? I can't answer that for sure, but I think it has something to do with the story Agent O sent me in one very long message I found rolled up along with my morning newspaper one day. The story relates the exciting and nearly unbelievable encounter between Agent O and the fabulously felonious Felicia (criminal mastermind extraordinaire). You can read the story and come to your own conclusions as to why Agent O thought it imperative that this information be delivered to kids around the world.

Enjoy Agent O's story, make the gadgets, learn the spy tricks, and most of all, always use your newfound spy skills for good. Meanwhile, I'll be hanging out in my hammock, waiting for my next message from Agent O.

Spy well,

Rain

HOW TO USE THIS BOOK

• Whenever you see this 🎩 while reading the story, look for Agent O's spy notes. They'll show you how to replicate spy tricks and techniques such as tailing your enemies, make cool spy gadgets like spy sunglasses, and create clever disguises.

• As you're reading this book, you'll come across messages in code. The codes contain information vital to figuring out what's happening in the story. Decode the messages and then use the codes in your own spy work.

• As an extra-special bonus, at the end of the book you'll find Agent O's Super Secret Spy Notebook.

A WORD OR TWO ON CODES

Many of the codes in this book are substitution codes. That means each letter of the actual message is replaced by one other letter, number, or symbol.

When cracking a code, work slowly. Copy the code onto a piece of paper, and leave a space between each line. Figure out one symbol at a time. When you know what letter a symbol represents, write it down above the symbol. Go through the entire message, and write that letter above the symbol each time it appears. Then figure out the next symbol. Here are some code-cracking tips:

• If the message has spaces between the coded words, look for single symbols. These are either A or I.

• E, H, S, and T are the four most common letters used in English words. Look for the four symbols that are used most often in the code. Substitute these letters for each one until something makes sense.

• The most common three-letter-word is THE.

• The most common double letters are OO, EE, PP, LL, TT, DD, SS, MM, and NN.

• Most words have at least one vowel. Try to figure out what symbol or letter represents A, E, I, O, and U.

• If you get frustrated by a code, flip to page 93 for help. If you totally give up, the deciphered codes are on page 94.

Hey There!

I'm Agent O.

I know you've never heard of me. I'm the world's most top-secret secret agent. If you knew who I was, I wouldn't be doing a very good job, would I?

And what is my job?

By day, I'm a full-time student at the Spy Academy. By night (and on weekends, holidays, and summer vacation), I'm a member of The Network—a top-secret organization dedicated to keeping the world safe from evildoers like this one ⟶

The Spy Academy is where aspiring spies gather to learn the tricks of the trade: spying on enemies, breaking codes, sending messages, concocting disguises, making cool gadgets, and that sort of thing. Unfortunately, extra-curricular spy activities are strictly forbidden by school policy.

Criminal mastermind extraordinaire—Felicia

If the headmaster were to find out that I spend my free time catching crooks as Agent O, I'd probably get suspended—or, if I'm lucky, stuck in detention for a very long time. (No one has ever escaped from the Detention Room.)

Nobody at The Network knows I'm a student at the Spy Academy. The few agents that have seen me think I'm just a really short adult. (I tell them it's easier to sneak around when you're small.)

You want to know more about me?

That information is classified. As soon as I entered the Spy Academy, all records of my former life were destroyed. This family photo is all that remains.

I hope that answers all your questions. Now, satisfy your curiosity about what it takes to be a great secret agent like me with this book. It'll teach you almost everything that I've learned so far. At great personal risk, I'm sharing my knowledge with you.

—Agent O

This photo has been altered to protect the identities of the innocent.

The Vanished Video Game

SPY LOG: 1.001

I WAS SITTING OUTSIDE A LITTLE RESTAURANT contemplating the details of my latest mission. I had been sent to recover a truckload of missing video games. Stashed inside one of the video game boxes was the contact information for The Network. The identities of every spy could be disclosed, and that meant their safety was threatened. It would be a complete disaster for everybody—especially me—if the information fell into the wrong hands. If the Headmaster at the Spy Academy found out that Agent O was one of her students, that would be the end of my career as the world's top-secret secret agent.

My last lead on the vanished video game had turned into a dead end. What would I do next?

Suddenly I was struck on the ear by something. It was no ordinary projectile. It was a **rubber band message**. One of my contacts at The Network thinks it's especially funny to shoot missives at me. To read the message, all I had to do was stretch out the rubber band and decode it. (Rubber band communications are always written in code.)

TAOCEULBEHTNINAMOWEHTWOLLOF

HINT: READ IT BACKWARD

Why is it that new leads always come in the middle of lunch? I didn't want to leave the delicious sandwich I was eating. But when duty calls, Agent O answers. With a little luck, the woman in the blue coat would lead me right to the missing video games.

RUBBER BAND MESSAGE

Making a rubber band message is easy.

WHAT YOU NEED
- Rubber band
- Book
- Pen

WHAT YOU DO

1. Stretch a rubber band around a book. The more you can stretch the band, the smaller your message will appear. (Be careful not to break the band.)

2. Write your coded message on it with the pen. Write as small as you can. Let the ink dry.

3. When your message is finished, take the rubber band off the book.

4. Shoot it at your contact—and don't forget to aim below the neck!

I **tailed** this mysterious stranger for some time. Eventually, she led me to a little house on the outskirts of town. Could it be the location of the stolen video games? There was only one way to find out—using more undercover spy operations, of course.

TAILING: Following your suspect and watching what she does
YOUR GOALS: Don't get caught. Figure out what your suspect is up to.
REQUIRED SKILL: Patience

A few tips:

- Know the area in which you're tailing. If you're familiar with the location, you can figure out where your suspect is headed.
- Don't stare at your suspect—just glance at her every now and again. Look at other people too. (This will throw off suspicion.)
- Move your eyes only when watching your suspect. From far away, it's easy to see somebody move her head, but nobody will notice if you just move your eyes.
- Don't stop and start when your suspect does. Stop randomly to look in store windows, tie your shoes, read a flyer, look at a map, rifle through your bag, etc.
- Stay 20 yards (about three store fronts) behind your suspect when you're in a crowded area.
- Stay 50 yards (about one block) behind your suspect when you're in an area with only a few other people.
- Bring a different-colored shirt or jacket and a hat with you. Reversible coats, hats, and sunglasses work well. Duck into an alley or store, or hide behind a car, to change into the new clothes and confuse your suspect.
- Avoid being photographed. You don't want anybody to have a record of what you look like or where you've been. Fake a sneezing fit to get out of the camera's viewfinder.
- Keep in the shadows at night. Don't step into bright lights.
- If you lose your suspect or think she has spotted you, give up the chase and try it another day.

THE FINE ART OF TAILING

ASSIGNMENTS FROM THE SPY ACADEMY

Mission: Tailing practice
Location: Crowded area, such as your school at lunchtime or the mall
Tools: None
Accomplices: One or more spy friends

Have your spy friend walk around and do interesting things. Tail him, noting what he does and when he does it. Afterward, compare observations. Did he notice you following him? Were there things he did that you didn't see? Did you do anything that attracted his notice or made him particularly suspicious of you?

For Advanced Students:
Gather a group of friends. Pick one to follow, but don't let anybody know which person you're tailing. See whether your friends can guess whom you followed when you're through.

SPY LOG: 1.003

I did a little 🎩 **recon work,** scoped out the lay of the land, and surreptitiously snapped a few pictures with my 🎩 **disguised camera.** The best place to set an observation post was behind the overgrown fence. Nobody ever came near it, and it was close enough that I could look in all the windows of the house to search for the missing video games.

THE RIDDLES OF RECON REVEALED

RECON: Observing a place for several days at many different times during the day (also known as reconnaissance)
YOUR GOALS: To find ways in and out of the building and out- smart security forces
REQUIRED SKILL: Awesome powers of observation

Carefully watch:
• All the traditional entrances and exits (doors)
• All the nontraditional entrances and exits (windows, chimneys, skylights, etc.)
• Anyplace you can hide
• Where the most activity in the building is
• Traffic patterns outside
• Traffic patterns inside
• Any regular delivery or maintenance work
• Guards

It helps to have a digital camera, but if you don't have one, you can do just as well with a notebook and a pen. (If you do have a digital camera, make a disguise for it.)

DISGUISED CAMERA

Disguise your camera to avoid attracting unwanted attention.

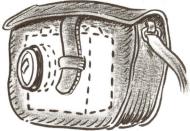

WHAT YOU NEED
- Camera
- Measuring tape
- Pen
- Old satchel, purse, or shoebox
- Scissors
- Clothes

WHAT YOU DO
1. Measure the width of the camera lens with the measuring tape.
2. Measure the distance from the base of the camera to the middle of the lens.
3. Use the measurement from step 2 and a pen to mark the place for a hole in the satchel. Measure from the bottom of the satchel, where the camera will sit.
4. With the scissors, poke a hole in the place you marked. Cut a hole slightly smaller than the size of the lens. Use the measurement from step 1.
5. Put the camera in the bag and poke the lens through the hole.
6. Stuff the clothes around the sides and back of the camera to hold it in place. Figure out how to push the button inconspicuously. Practice in front of a mirror—if you can fool yourself, you can fool anybody. You won't be able to look through the viewfinder before taking a picture, so practice first.

SPY LOG: 1.004

Before I did any more surveillance, I needed to let my contacts at The Network know what was happening. That way, should anything go awry, they'd know where to rescue me. (Not that anything was going to go wrong—I'm way too sneaky for that.) Nonetheless, proper spy protocol demanded I send them a message.

SPY LOG: 1.005

The first step in contacting The Network was to code the message. Here it is:

Th eh id eo ut is on th en or th si de of to wn. I'm co mi ng ba ck to mo rr ow wi th ap er is co pe to fi gu re ou ti fs he ha st he ga me s.

HINT: REMOVE THE SPACES, THEN PUT THEM BACK WHERE THEY BELONG.

I wrote a rough draft of the coded message on a piece of scrap paper with a pencil because I was going to write the real one in **invisible ink.** Once you start writing with invisible ink, you can't read what you've written.

INVISIBLE INK

There are many ways to make invisible ink. You can usually find everything you need for this one in your kitchen.

WHAT YOU NEED
- Lemon juice
- Cup
- Thin paintbrush
- Paper
- Lightbulb

WHAT YOU DO

1. Pour the lemon juice into a cup. Dip the paintbrush into the lemon juice. Use the paintbrush to write your secret message on the paper.

2. When the paintbrush starts to dry, repeat step 1. Do this until you've written the entire message.

3. Let the message dry and rinse out the paintbrush.

4. To make the invisible ink appear, hold the message over the top of a lightbulb and turn on the light. The lemon juice will turn brown.

The next step was to disguise the message as something no one but my contact would ever think to look at: a leaf! That way, any enemy agents that might be lurking about wouldn't be able to intercept it and mess with my plans.

LEAF DISGUISE

These clever containers take a couple of days to dry, so make several at a time.

WHAT YOU NEED
- Leaf
- Pencil
- String
- Paper

WHAT YOU DO
1. Find a green leaf that is at least 2 inches wide. Roll it around the pencil.
2. Tie up the leaf tube with a piece of string. Let it dry out completely.
3. Slip the leaf off the pencil and remove the string. The leaf will hold its shape.
4. Write a message on a piece of paper. Roll the paper into a tight tube and slip it inside the leaf cover. (If you want, you can tie the message with a piece of string first.)

SPY LOG: 1.006

After writing my coded message in invisible ink and disguising it as a leaf, I couldn't just hand it to my contact. You never know who might be watching, and one must never do anything that could reveal the identity of a secret contact. This is more than merely a professional courtesy—everyone's safety depends on the secrecy of The Network.

I had to make a dead drop at the zoo.

DEAD DROP

DEAD DROP: A prearranged place to leave a message

YOUR GOAL: To secretly pass a message to your contact

REQUIRED SKILLS: Proper planning and choosing an excellent location

To use a dead drop, leave a coded message there for your contact to pick up. Make a signpost so that he'll know there's a message waiting.

The perfect spot for a dead drop should meet the following criteria:

- It is completely unnoticeable.
- No one will look for something else there and accidentally find the message.
- No one can see you putting stuff there. (Don't forget to check for tall buildings. People on the upper stories may be able to see you.)
- You can hide or pretend there's another reason to be there if someone interrupts the dead drop.

Here are a few good places to stash messages:

- Under a rock
- Underneath a root or bush
- In the cracks of a park bench
- Stuck to the bottom of a desk
- Beneath couch cushions or the base of a lamp
- In the soil of a potted plant
- Taped to the bottom of a table
- Inside the hollowed-out stomach of a snowman

ASSIGNMENTS FROM THE SPY ACADEMY

Mission: Create unique locations for dead drops

Location: Your school

Tools: Secret messages, tape

Accomplices: At least one contact

Use the following locations as dead drops for your secret messages:

- The underside of a drinking fountain
- A book in the library
- The bottom of a desk
- The bottom of the teacher's desk
- Underneath a trash can
- In the rolled-up blinds of a window shade

- In a fence with a hollow pole
- Inside a decorative birdhouse (not one that birds actually live in)

When approaching the dead drop, remember:

- Never use the most direct route to your dead drop.
- Make sure nobody's watching when you approach your dead drop. Even the most harmless-seeming observer could be an enemy spy.
- Don't visit your dead drop more than necessary.

SPY LOG: 1007

My contact and I had picked out five different places to stash the message at the zoo. I left him **a signpost** to tell him that there was a message and which dead drop it was at.

SIGNPOST: A signal that lets your contact know there's a message at the dead drop

YOUR GOALS: To figure out an unobtrusive signal that can't be accidentally set

REQUIRED SKILLS: Proper planning and a good memory

Stash the message at the dead drop. Make a signpost with a piece of chalk. Your contact will see the signpost, destroy i and collect the message. When you pass by later and see th signpost is gone, you'll know the message has been collecte

Places to leave chalk signposts:

- The base of a rock
- On a monument
- On a fence
- On a tree

How not to leave chalk signposts:

- Don't put them on the sidewalk. People will erase them with their feet.
- Don't leave a chalk signpost when it's about to rain.
- Don't be obvious about it. Pretend to tie your shoe.

Here are some examples of chalk signposts. If you have more than one dead drop, the signpost can direct you to the right one.

— gnı tıa wega ssem	≀ kee rce ht ott xe
= egas semo n	≀≀ ee rt ehtn ı
X de nıu rpo rd	

HINT: IGNORE THE SPACING AND READ THE MESSAGE BACKWARD.

SPY LOG: 1008

Later that day, I strolled by the bench. My contact had erased the signpost I left, so I knew he had successfully retrieved the message. It was time to continue the preparations for my surveillance mission.

ASSIGNMENTS FROM THE SPY ACADEMY

Mission: Create signposts out of ordinary items
Location: Kitchen
Tools: Refrigerator magnets
Accomplices: One or more contacts

Move a special magnet from one side of the fridge to the other. The position of the magnet indicates where to collect the message at the dead drop.

For Advanced Students:
Move all the magnets to throw counterspies off your track.

SPY LOG: 1.009

My plan was to return to the lady-in-blue's house and use the cover of the over-grown fence to hide myself while I peered into the windows, searching for the stolen video games. Sticking my head over the top of the fence would give away my position. I needed a gadget that would let me look over the fence without being seen. And that meant making 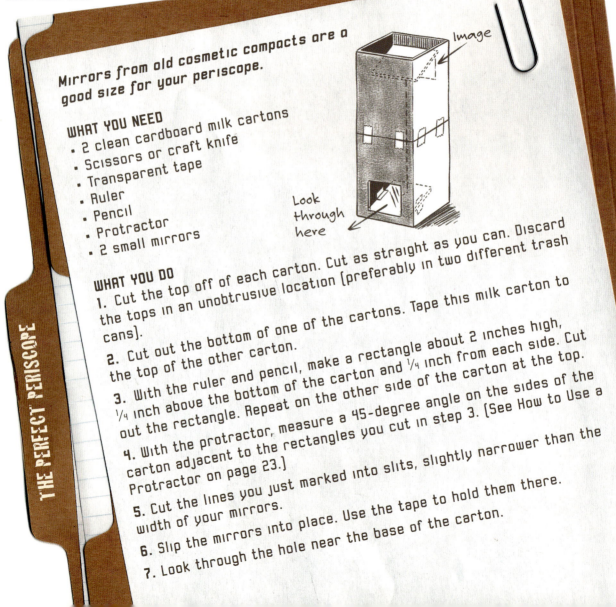 **a periscope,** which is a lot easier than stealing one from a submarine. For one thing, all you need is a couple of milk cartons and mirrors.

Mirrors from old cosmetic compacts are a good size for your periscope.

Image

Look through here

WHAT YOU NEED
- 2 clean cardboard milk cartons
- Scissors or craft knife
- Transparent tape
- Ruler
- Pencil
- Protractor
- 2 small mirrors

WHAT YOU DO

1. Cut the top off of each carton. Cut as straight as you can. Discard the tops in an unobtrusive location (preferably in two different trash cans).

2. Cut out the bottom of one of the cartons. Tape this milk carton to the top of the other carton.

3. With the ruler and pencil, make a rectangle about 2 inches high, 1/4 inch above the bottom of the carton and 1/4 inch from each side. Cut out the rectangle. Repeat on the other side of the carton at the top.

4. With the protractor, measure a 45-degree angle on the sides of the carton adjacent to the rectangles you cut in step 3. (See How to Use a Protractor on page 23.)

5. Cut the lines you just marked into slits, slightly narrower than the width of your mirrors.

6. Slip the mirrors into place. Use the tape to hold them there.

7. Look through the hole near the base of the carton.

THE PERFECT PERISCOPE

HOW TO USE A PROTRACTOR

A protractor is shaped like the letter D. There should be a hole or two intersecting lines in the middle of the straight part. Line up the hole with the corner of the milk carton. Line up on the 45-degree mark, extending from the corner to the middle of the carton.

SPY LOG: 1.010

With my periscope completed and The Network contacted, it was time to finish this mission. I packed up my spy gear and headed out.

SPY LOG: 1.011

Once situated behind the fence, I carefully raised the periscope. Busted! There was the woman in blue with several burly henchmen and a huge pile of video games. They were haphazardly tossing the games about. I took some quick pictures with my disguised camera. I wanted photographic evidence to send to my contact. While I snapped pictures, I wondered what exactly this mysterious woman was up to.

Was she really searching for The Network contact information? If she was, she wasn't going about it very systematically. Obviously, the coded video game would be marked in some way so that we could find it again later. The logical thing to do would be to separate all the video boxes that look slightly different from the rest. That way, there'd be a lot less to sort through.

As I watched through my periscope, I began to suspect that she had a far more nefarious plan for the 42,670 identical video games. The only way to find out was through further observation…and asking my fellow spies for information.

It was time to let my contact know I'd located the missing video games. The Network would send a team to retrieve the contact information on it. I could've snuck in there and grabbed it myself, but it was far too dangerous. If I got caught, the Headmaster at the Spy Academy would put an end to Agent O. (And she'd put me in detention for breaking school rules, too.)

This is the secret message I wrote to The Network with 🎩 **wet pencil writing** (read it quickly before it dries):

Szeznzd izn a sznzezazkzy
azgzeznzt tzo rzeztzrzizezvze tzhz
e vziz dzezo gzazmze wziztzh
tzhze iznzfzo ozn izt.
Eznzczlzozszezd azrze tzhze
pzhzoztzozs ozf tzhze hzizdze-
zozuzt fzrzozm mzy rzezczozn
mzizszszizozn. Lzezazvze tzhze
rzezszt ozf tzhze vzizdzezo
gzazmzezs tzhzezrze. I wzanzt tzo
fzizgzuzrze ozuzt wzhzazt tzhzizs
wzozmzazn izs uzp tzo. Szeznzd
mze aznzy iznzfzo yzozu hzazvze
ozn hzezr.   **HINT: REMOVE THE ZS.**

WET PENCIL WRITING

Use a pencil to make invisible ink.

WHAT YOU NEED
- Water
- 2 sheets of paper
- Newspaper
- Pencil

WHAT YOU DO
1. Wet one piece of paper and put it on top of the newspaper.

2. Put the second piece of paper on top of the first. Use the pencil to write your secret message. Press hard. Remove the top sheet of paper and get rid of it.

3. As the paper dries, the pencil lines will vanish. To make them appear again, wet the paper with cold water.

Note: Make sure your decoy message is written in pencil. Otherwise the ink will bleed when you get the paper wet.

SPY LOG: 1.012

I needed to send the pictures I took during my recon mission as well as the secret message. Then the team The Network sent to retrieve the video games would know exactly where to go.

I hid the photos in a 🎩 **CD case**. To protect it for shipping, I crumpled up a whole bunch of pieces of plain white paper. I folded the secret message in half, crumpled it up, and stuck it in the box too. When my contact unpacked the CD, he'd notice that one of the pieces of paper had been folded in half before being crumpled. That would be the piece of paper he'd test for a secret message.

On the return address of the package, I wrote "Helen Ortega, 2nd Ave West" for the return address. The letters "H," "O," and the number "2" would let my contact know to use water to reveal the code.

HELEN ORTEGA
2ND AVE WEST
NY, NY 10011

CD CASE HOLDER

The best place to hide anything in a CD is between the disk tray and the back cover.

Coded message

WHAT YOU NEED
- CD with jewel case, liner notes, and a printed cover in the back
- Photos or message

WHAT YOU DO
1. Open the CD case. Remove the CD and set it aside.
2. Gently pry out the plastic insert that holds the CD. Start at the top left corner, next to the spine. Work slowly and use your fingernails a lot. Don't break the insert.
3. Put the photo or message in the back of the jewel case. Snap the plastic insert back into place. Put the CD back.

SPY LOG 1.013

Three days later, I found an empty root beer can in my trash. Not being a root beer drinker, I was immediately suspicious. I fished it out of the trash and brought it into the kitchen.

Empty soda cans are classic message covers at the Spy Academy. I was kind of surprised that an adult spy would still use one.

This is the message I found in the can:

HINT: REVERSE THE LETTERS IN EACH PAIR TO FORM THE WORDS.

HT GE MA HE SA EB NE ER RT EI EV D. PS EI AS OR NU TD
EH OWLR HD VA FE LI SE NO HT WE MO NA. EH NR MA IE FS
LE CI AI. HS SE CA IR IM AN ML SA ET MR NI D. EK PE NA
YE OE HN RE.

Instead of apprehending this "Felicia," The Network decided to keep an eye on her to see what her next move would be. And how did 42,669 identical video games fit into the schemes of a criminal mastermind? It was now my job to find out.

SODA CAN COVER-UP

Soda cans are convenient and inconspicuous message covers.

WHAT YOU NEED
- Empty soda can
- Message
- Can opener

WHAT YOU DO
1. Rinse out the soda can. Let it dry.
2. Roll up the message and slip it inside the can. Put it in the dead drop spot for your contact.
3. To open the can, use the can opener to remove the top.
4. Flip the can upside down. The message will drop out.

The Missing Megabytes

SPY LOG 2.001

I KEPT TABS ON FELICIA AND HER HENCHMEN after school and on weekends. I tailed Felicia to the Culinary Institute and discovered she was taking cheese-making classes every Tuesday. So the next Tuesday I snuck into her headquarters and hacked into the computer. I discovered that she and her lackeys were also taking computer programming classes online. How odd. Perhaps they had discovered that crime really doesn't pay, and they were trying to live as law-abiding citizens.

One morning the city newspaper arrived on my doorstep. Since I don't have a subscription to the paper, I was certain there had to be a message in it somewhere. Sure enough, the crossword puzzle had already been filled in. Someone at The Network was sending me intelligence in **crossword code.**

HINT: READ ONE WORD DOWN PER COLUMN.

Nobody looks at crossword puzzles that are filled in, so they're the perfect place for leaving messages.

WHAT YOU NEED
- Crossword puzzle
- Pen
- Message

WHAT YOU DO
1. Write each letter of your message in the blocks going down. Write only one word for each column.
2. Write random letters and unimportant words in the rest of the blank spaces.
3. Leave the crossword puzzle on a table in a café or on a park bench for your contact to pick up.

SPY LOG 2.002

It was time to figure out why Felicia's henchmen stole a laptop from Applegate University. On my way out the door, I grabbed my favorite **spy trench coat.** I had added extra pockets to hold all of my gadgets.

You can add spy storage to any trench coat or jacket with a needle and thread. [Ask permission before making holes in your good coat, though.]

WHAT YOU NEED
- Adult helper
- Seam ripper
- Old trench coat
- Measuring tape
- Scissors
- Fabric
- Pins
- Needle and thread

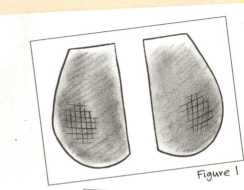

Figure 1

WHAT YOU DO

1. Use the seam ripper to open a 4-inch slit in the side seam of the coat where you want the pocket.

2. Use the scissors to cut out two pieces of fabric following figure 1. The opening of the pocket should be 4½ inches wide.

Figure 2

3. Pin the pocket pieces together. Thread the needle, tie a knot in the end, and sew around the outside edge of the pocket. Leave about ¼ inch between the edge of the fabric and the stitches. Leave the opening of the pocket unstitched. [See figure 2.]

4. Turn the trench coat inside out. Pin the open edges of the pocket to the opening in the seam. [See figure 3.]

5. Sew the open edges of the pocket to each side of the coat seam.

6. Turn the coat right side out and push the new pocket through to the inside of the coat.

7. Follow steps 1 through 5 to make as many pockets as you want.

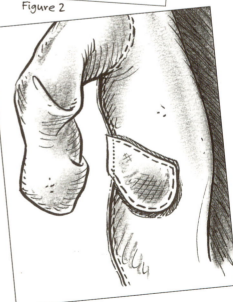

Figure 3

SPY LOG 2.003

There were no signs of life at Felicia's headquarters, so I scoped out all the places—such as video arcades and laundromats—where the henchmen of criminal master-minds might congregate. But there was no sign of Felicia's flunkies.

While at the laundromat, I picked up a copy of the newspaper. I decided to research the problem of Felicia and the stolen laptop by reading the classified ads. Felicia's henchmen needed to get the laptop to their boss. Telephone lines are too easy to bug, so the henchmen might send Felicia a message through the classified ads. I quickly scanned the ads looking for something suspicious.

This is what I found:

For Sale: Rooftop apartment. 2130 W 34th Street.

No appointments before 10 P.M.

That seemed strange. Who would go apartment hunting at 10 P.M.? I suspected the ad was an attempt by Felicia's henchmen to set up a meeting. I headed for the corner of 21st Avenue and 34th Street.

SPY LOG 2.004

I found the apartment supposedly for sale—and guess who appeared in the window at 9:57? Felicia! Suddenly, a light started flashing from a rooftop nearby. I pulled out my 🎩 **spy writing kit** to scribble down the 🎩 **light signals** in order to decode it later. The henchmen signaling Felicia were using 🎩 **Morse code.**

HINT: —··· ·—· ·· —· ——· = BRING

```
·—— ·   ·—— ··  ·—·· ·—··   —··· ·—· ··  —· ——·   —  ···· ·   —  ···· ·
·—·· ·— ·—·  — ——— ·——·   — ———— —   — ···· ·   —··· ·— —·—· —·—
·—· ——— ——— —   ——— ··—·   ——— ··—·   — ···· ·   —·—· ·— —·
—·· —·—— ···  ···· ·— —·— —·—  ·—  —  —  ·—— ———
```

So the laptop would not be handed over this evening as I expected. Apparently Felicia had expected the same, and she didn't appear to be very happy about not getting the laptop. Henchmen are notorious for messing up the exacting plans of criminal masterminds. But now I would have the opportunity to observe tomorrow's meeting.

SPY WRITING KIT

Use your spy kit to stash note-taking supplies or anything else you want.

WHAT YOU NEED
- Matchbox with matches
- Scissors
- Cardboard
- Glue
- Mini-spy gadgets

WHAT YOU DO
1. Use the scissors to cut a piece of cardboard so that it will fit snuggly inside the matchbox drawer.
2. Glue matchsticks to the piece of cardboard. Set it aside and let the glue dry.
3. Fill the matchbox with mini-spy gadgets, such as a sharpened pencil stub, wax, a rubber band, paper, or a leaf code hider.
4. Put the matchstick cover you made in step 2 on top of your supplies and close the matchbox.

MORSE CODE

Morse code was invented in 1844. Each letter in the alphabet is broken down into different signals using dots and dashes. That means you can use Morse code with anything that can make a dot or dash. Light and sound both work well. To keep your communications secret, make up your own versions of Morse code. Assign a different sequence of dots and dashes to every letter. For instance:

Morse Code: A = .—
Your Code: A = ..

Don't use ... or ——— as any of your code letters. This signal is SOS and it's a universal distress sign. If your coded message places these signals next to each other, hordes of well-meaning people will come running to your rescue. That'll blow your cover faster than you can say:

.——— ..— ... —   —.— .. —.. —.. .. —. —.!

LIGHT SIGNALS

To send a light signal, all you need is a source of light and a way to block it.

WHAT YOU NEED
• Flashlight or light and curtain
• Morse code

WHAT YOU DO
1. Turn the flashlight on. Count to one for a dot and two for a dash. Turn the flashlight off.

2. If you have the kind of curtains that roll up, pull a curtain up and down as if it's stuck. Pull it halfway down for a dot and all the way down for a dash. Close the curtain between each signal.

3. If you have the kind of curtains that pull apart in the center, pull them closed. Lift one corner up. Count to one for a dot and two for a dash. Let the corner fall.

SPY LOG 2.005

I made it to Camilla's Candy Shack a few minutes before 2:00 P.M. I wanted to check out the place (and get some of Camilla's famous peppermint candies). I was in luck. One of the walls of the back room was made out of frosted glass. It was going to be really easy to 🔍 **see through the wall.** If Felicia wasn't there but the laptop was, I could probably steal it right back from her incompetent lackeys.

SEEING THROUGH WALLS

You can see through a wall with a piece of tape—if you have the right kind of wall.

WHAT YOU NEED
- Scissors
- Clear packing tape
- Frosted glass wall

WHAT YOU DO
1. Use the scissors to cut off a 3-inch piece of tape.
2. Stick the tape to the frosted-glass wall at a height you can easily see.
3. Look through the tape. Move it if you need to.

Drat! Felicia was already in there with her henchmen! And whatever they had on the table looked suspiciously like the missing laptop. I pulled out my water glass so I could 🎩 **listen through the wall**, hoping I might discover where the laptop was being taken. Then I could send another agent from The Network to steal it back.

Excellent! I knew exactly where the laptop was going to be next. Unfortunately, I was so busy memorizing that last bit of information that I didn't pay enough attention to the footsteps.

Somebody was opening the door. Uh-oh. I'd been spotted.

I got out of Camilla's Candy Shack as quickly as I could.

This trick is a classic—it's simple and it always works.

WHAT YOU NEED
- Drinking glass*
- Wall

*The glass must be made of real glass. A tall glass with thin sides will let you hear the most.

WHAT YOU DO
1. Stick the mouth of the drinking glass on the wall.
2. Press your ear against the base of the drinking glass.
3. Listen.

LISTENING THROUGH WALLS

I slipped on my 🎩 **spyglasses** and glanced in the mirrors. Sure enough, one of Felicia's flunkies was coming after me. It shouldn't be too hard to 🎩 **shake this tail,** though.

SPYGLASSES

A good spy has eyes on the back of her head...or at least pretends to! Use a pair of spyglasses to see behind yourself.

WHAT YOU NEED
- Large, dark mirrored sunglasses
- 2 mirrors, 1 x ½ inch each*
- Masking tape
- Hot glue gun and glue sticks

*You can find tiny mirrors in most craft stores. If you can't find them, glass stores will cut mirrors to any size you want.

WHAT YOU DO

1. Find a pair of sunglasses to use for this project. A pair with lenses a little bit wider than your face will work best.

2. Position the mirrors on the outside edges of the sunglasses (see illustration). Use the masking tape to hold them in place while you try them on. Experiment with the position of the mirrors until you can see what's behind you by turning your head slightly.

3. When you're happy with the placement of the mirrors, remove the masking tape. Use the hot glue gun to glue the mirrors in place. Let the glue dry.

4. Practice wearing your rearview glasses. Figure out how to move your head around so you can see behind you. Be subtle—jerky, obvious head movements will let enemy spies know that there's something fishy going on.

Note: Don't wear these sunglasses in the rain or after dark. It will blow your disguise.

HOW TO SHAKE A TAIL

Sometimes even the best spy slips up and gets followed. No matter what you do, don't lead the enemy to your destination.

WHAT YOU NEED
- Your wits
- Every opportunity around you

WHAT YOU DO
1. Never look directly at the enemy spy. You don't want him to know that you know that he's following you.

2. Watch for when a group of people or a car blocks you from the enemy spy's sight. Then change direction or slip down a side street when he can't see you.

3. Casually walk into a store. Leave by the back exit or hide in a bathroom or dressing room until the coast is clear.

4. Duck down an alley and pull out your disguise shirt. Put it on. Leave the way you came.

5. If all else fails, go to a completely wrong spot and pretend you are collecting a message. The next day, you can go back to that spot and leave a carefully coded and completely false message there. Then, the enemy spy will pick it up and think he has the real message.

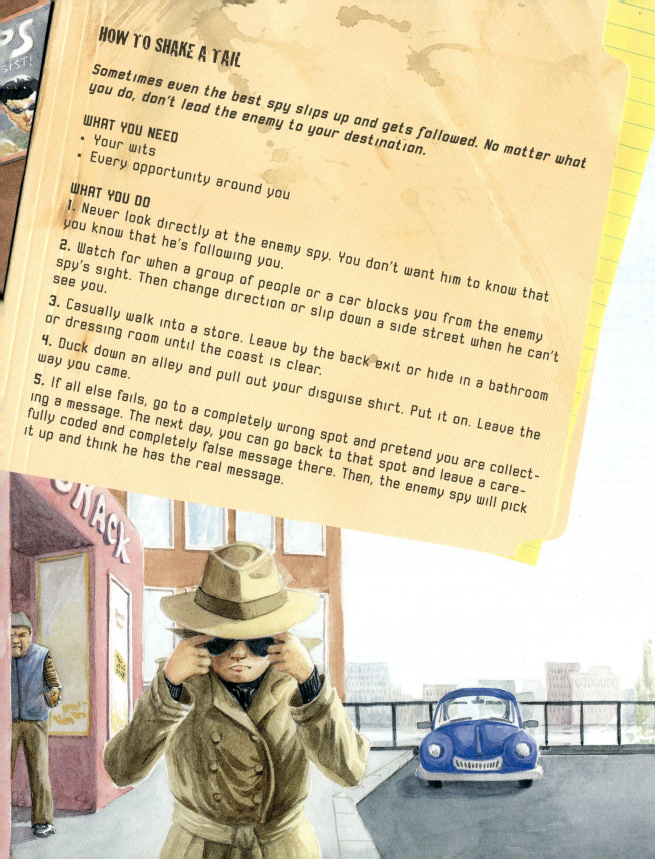

37

SPY LOG 2.007

As I ducked down an alley, I glimpsed another one of Felicia's flunkies in the rearview mirror part of my spy glasses. Interesting...it would appear that Felicia had instructed several of her henchmen to follow me. **A multiple-agent tail** requires a considerable amount of forethought and cooperation to work. I doubted that those lackluster lackeys had the skills to pull it off. They should be easy to lose.

MULTIPLE-AGENT TAIL: When more than one spy is tailing a suspect

YOUR GOAL: To keep an eye on the suspect without arousing suspicion

REQUIRED SKILLS: Proper planning, teamwork, and good body language signals

Having just one agent tail a suspect can make the suspect suspicious. A person tends to notice when somebody has been following her for a while. But if different people take up the trail at different times, your suspect will suspect nothing!

This is how you work with multiple agents to follow somebody:

- Ahead of time, study the area you think the person will be traveling through
- Pick out specific areas for each agent to cover. If you have enough agents, this area shouldn't be more than a couple of blocks.
- Each agent will be stationed somewhere in his or her area. When the subject leaves one agent's area, the next agent takes over.
- Use body language signals to communicate with your fellow agents.
  For example:
  - Tug on left ear: Go straight
  - Scratch head: Take a right
  - Fiddle with button: Lost him
  - Tie shoelace: Take a left
  - Finger on temple: Suspect is suspicious
  - Left hand on hip: Break off pursuit

I hunkered down behind the dumpster and took off my trench coat and hat. I wadded them up and put them in what I hoped was the least dirty part of the dumpster. I'd come back and retrieve them later if I could.

A good spy never leaves home without a  **back-up disguise.** I was wearing a gray sweater under my trench coat. My new look would confuse Felicia's henchmen enough to let me slip away unnoticed.

BACK-UP DISGUISES

BACK-UP DISGUISES: The easiest way to fool a person tailing you
YOUR GOAL: To disguise yourself in a hurry
REQUIRED SKILLS: Proper planning, magician-like reflexes

Here are two options:

1. Wear a reversible jacket or shirt.
2. Carry a lightweight shirt in your pocket or backpack. Go somewhere you can't be seen: for example, down an alley, behind a car, or around a corner. Change your shirt. Stash your old shirt somewhere inconspicuous.

If you have to hide your face in a hurry, try these:

- Carry a handkerchief in your pocket. Pull it out and pretend to blow your nose in it. Cover as much of your face as possible.
- Drop some money on the ground and stoop down to pick it up.
- Tie your shoelace.
- Search through your backpack or purse.
- Stick your nose in a newspaper or book.
- Wrap a scarf around your face (as long as it's cold out).

SPY LOG: 2.008

As soon as I got home, I peeked out my bedroom window and checked the street below. One of Felicia's henchmen was standing outside my building. I hadn't lost my tail, and I had made one of the biggest mistakes a spy can make: I had under-estimated the intelligence of my enemy. Now I needed to think my way out of this mess. And on top of it all, I had an appointment to keep. My contact from The Network was waiting for me at the art museum. I was supposed to pass her the information I had learned about the whereabouts of the laptop.

Perhaps I could lure Felicia's henchmen into picking up a fake message while my contact retrieved the real one. I brainstormed this plan:

1. Write out a fake message to pass to the enemy agents.
2. Make sure the enemy agents follow me to the meeting spot.
3. Set up a decoy so they think I don't think they're following me.
4. Pretend to make a dead drop so the enemy agent who follows me will collect the fake message.
5. Give the real message to my contact.

SPY LOG 2.009

To let my contact know where to look for the message, I made a 🎩 **signal bracelet.** We had agreed to pass each other in the Impressionist wing of the art museum. The color of my bracelet would tell her that the message was in my hat. She'd be able to collect the message without Felicia's henchmen noticing.

You can carry around multiple bracelets with you. Each one indicates a separate code. Practice secretly switching bracelets so that you can change the code when you need to.

WHAT YOU NEED
- Scissors
- Elastic thread*
- Masking tape
- Several colors of beads
- Color code

* You can find this at bead stores.

WHAT YOU DO
1. Cut a piece of elastic thread 12 inches long. Put a piece of masking tape on one end. (This will keep the beads from falling off as you string it.)

2. String enough beads of the same color onto the bracelet until it is long enough to fit. It should be snug enough to fit without flopping around, but not so tight that the elastic is stretched out.

3. Carefully take the masking tape off the elastic. You can cut it off if you want.

4. Hold both ends of the thread and tie a square knot (see figures 1 and 2).

5. Make a bracelet for each color of your code.
For example:

RED: Danger
YELLOW: Message waiting
BLUE: No message
GREEN: All clear
Purple: Come back later
BLACK: Code is broken

Figure 1   Figure 2

SPY LOG 2.010

I prepared a 🕶 **wax pencil message** to leave for the henchmen to find. I made sure the code wasn't too easy to break. Felicia might realize that the message was a trick if the code was too simple, and I certainly wasn't going to underestimate my opponent's intelligence again. That's what got me into this mess in the first place.

This is what the message said:

FPE LEI CWI AND OTE SWN ORT HEA VQE IZT. IPM BWE IHN GOW AIT CVH EXD. MNI SJS IMO NIA BRO RIT EFD.

HINT: REMOVE THE MIDDLE LETTER FROM EACH GROUP.

I folded up the fake message, put it in an envelope, and stuck it in the pocket of my yellow rain jacket. I missed my trench coat. I'd retrieve it on the way to the museum.

Writing with wax makes a message that's nearly invisible.

WHAT YOU NEED
- Candle with dried wax drips
- Paper
- Chalk dust, cocoa powder, or instant coffee

WHAT YOU DO

1. Break off a wax drip from the candle. Roll it in your hands to warm it up. If you'd like, you can make it into more of a pencil shape as it softens.

2. Write the secret message on the paper using the wax pencil.

3. To make the message appear, shake the chalk dust, cocoa powder, or instant coffee over the paper. The chalk dust will stick to the wax, making the message legible.

WAX PENCIL MESSAGE

SPY LOG 2.011

I made some chemist's invisible ink for the real message for my contact. In this message, I put the information I discovered by eavesdropping at Camilla's Candy Shack.

HINT: PUT THE SECOND ROW OF LETTERS IN BETWEEN THE FIRST.

TEATPSENTKNOHAROT.YUHUDESBOEREETRMHTIDOKRNHLFAYIEFELNH.

HLPOIBIGAETTEIPR.OSOLBALTRTIVIFOTEHRLCEOTEETNTMATRUC.

I folded the note into a tiny square. Then, I got a special hat out of the closet and hid the message in the ribbon that goes around the inside of the hat. (My contact has the exact same hat.) I put on my signal bracelet and the hat. I was almost ready for the rendezvous.

You can find all the ingredients for this invisible ink in your kitchen.

WHAT YOU NEED
- Tablespoon
- Baking soda
- Water
- Cup
- Small paintbrush
- White paper
- Pen
- Grape juice or lightbulb

WHAT YOU DO

1. Mix 1 tablespoon of baking soda with 1 tablespoon of water in the cup.

2. Use the paintbrush to write your message on the piece of paper. (Because your writing will be invisible, work out your coded message on a piece of scrap paper first.)

3. Get more ink on the paintbrush whenever the paper stops getting wet. If you're writing slowly, you may want to stir the baking soda-water mixture again.

4. Let the message dry completely. Write a decoy message in pen on top if you want.

5. To make the ink appear, paint over the message with grape juice. You can also hold the message over a turned-on lightbulb.

CHEMIST'S INVISIBLE INK

43

A good decoy allows you to be in two places at once.

WHAT YOU NEED

- Hat
- Windowsill
- Wide packing tape

WHAT YOU DO

1. Put on the hat. Walk around your room for a while. Make sure you pass in front of the window several times so that the people watching you see you wearing the hat.

2. Sneak up to the windowsill. Kneel behind it so that only the top of your hat is visible. This will make it look like you're trying to see out the window without being seen.

3. Slide the hat off your head carefully. Balance it on the ledge of the windowsill.

4. Use the packing tape to affix the hat to the ledge. Stick one end of a 6-inch strip of tape to the inside of the hat and tape the other end to the wall. For extra protection, put a piece of tape over the brim and onto the windowsill. Be sneaky about applying the tape, though!

5. Crawl out of the room on your hands and knees until you are well out of sight of any windows or doors.

MAKING A DECOY

SPY LOG 2.012

This situation called for a 🎩 **decoy.** I taped my hat to the windowsill where the henchmen would see it. When I left the building, deliberately making sure they spotted me, the henchmen would follow and think they had outsmarted me. They would never suspect that I wanted them to follow me.

This trick will work on any door.

WHAT YOU NEED
- Door
- Toothpick

WHAT YOU DO

1. Close the door. Stick the toothpick in the crack so it's just above the doorknob. Stick it about halfway in.

2. Break off the toothpick so it's flush with the door. Put the broken end in your pocket. Make sure you can't see the other end in the door.

3. When you return, see whether the toothpick is on the floor or still jammed in the door frame. If it's on the floor, you know someone has invaded your space. If it's still in the door, check to make sure that your broken half of toothpick matches the half that's there. A smart spy would have replaced your toothpick. No two toothpicks break the same way, so you'll know whether it's your toothpick in the door. If they don't fit together, someone was in your room.

Once I had crawled carefully out the door, I rigged it with a **toothpick alarm.** That way I would know whether a henchman had searched my room while I was gone. When you're a spy, you can pretty much expect someone to search your room whenever you leave. The important thing is to know when someone has, and what he found while he was there.

SPY LOG 2.013

When I walked back to the alley to retrieve my trench coat, I made sure a henchman was following me. What would be the point in leaving a fake message if no one saw me do it?

As I put on the trench coat, I noticed an odd bulge in one of the pockets. I'd investigate it later. For now, I stuffed the fake message for Felicia into a different pocket and headed to the rendezvous.

THE RULES OF RENDEZVOUS

RENDEZVOUS: Giving your contact a message with lots of people around
YOUR GOAL: Not to let anyone notice that you've passed a message
REQUIRED SKILLS: Sneakiness, a great poker face, and a little forethought

The rendezvous is a face-to-face meeting with your contact done so sneakily that nobody—not even the enemy spy tailing you—knows it's taking place.

You and your contact agree on where and how the rendezvous is going to be made beforehand. The trick to a successful rendezvous is to act just like everything is perfectly normal. Observe what people do in everyday situations and figure out how you can turn these situations into message-passing moments.

You have two options for a rendezvous:
1. Exchange an item with the message hidden inside it.
2. Walk past your contact wearing or holding something that is the message.

THE OLD SWITCHEROO

This trick is absolutely the classic way to exchange an item. You and your contact have two identical items, such as a hat, bag, or coat. Put your item down somewhere. Your contact puts her item down close to yours. When you leave, you take hers instead of your own.

VISUAL MESSAGES

Assign different colors or items a code word or phrase. For instance, wearing a scarf might mean "Danger! Enemy spies are following me." When your contact passes you at the rendezvous point wearing a scarf, you've been given the message.

At the museum I left my trench coat and hat (with the hidden message for my contact) in the cloakroom. My contact would be wearing an identical hat. When we passed each other in the Impressionist wing, she would see the color of my bracelet and know how to retrieve the message: On her way out, she would take my hat from the cloakroom and leave hers in its place. When she got home, she'd find the message, decode it, and contact The Network about the whereabouts of the laptop.

THE FINE ART of DISGUISE

PERFORMING ARTS of CHINA

SPY LOG 2.015

So, the real message was being picked up by my contact. Now to plant the fake message...I pulled the envelope and some 🎩 **tape** out of my pocket. Then I sat down near a fountain and stuck the envelope in a conspicuous spot. I made sure the henchman was looking when I did it.

STICKY SITUATIONS

YOUR GOAL: To stick something somewhere at any time

REQUIRED SKILLS: The ability to identify and carry anything that's sticky

Ingenuity and readily available sticky stuff are the keys to leaving secret messages. It's fairly easy to carry a glue stick around in your pocket, but here are a few suggestions of other sticky stuff: gum, dental wax, and nacho cheese (the nasty kind you find at concession stands).

Ways to store tape:

• Wrap transparent tape around a pencil or water bottle. Overlap several layers of it. Everything but the first layer you put on will stay sticky.

• Make a duct tape bracelet. Cut a long strip and stick the sticky sides together. Wrap it around your wrist and tape it together. Then wrap more layers of duct tape around the bracelet. Peel off the duct tape when you need to use it.

SPY LOG 2.016

When I got home, I checked the door to see whether the toothpick alarm had been tripped. It had been! So someone had been in my room while I was out. I checked around to see what had been looked at. It's a good thing I always keep my room 🎩 **intruder-proofed.** My top-secret stuff was undisturbed.

INTRUDER-PROOF YOUR ROOM

YOUR GOAL: To organize your room so that you can tell whether someone has been snooping.

REQUIRED SKILLS: Cleanliness, organization, and a good memory

THE DRESSER

If your clothes are messy or scattered around your room, you won't be able to tell whether somebody has been looking through them. Fold your clothes in a certain way. For instance, fold the left arm of your shirt over and then fold the right arm over the top. If your clothes are rumpled, reordered, or folded the wrong way, you'll know someone has been in your dresser.

YOUR DESK

Stack all of your papers in an interesting pattern detectable only by you. Put each piece of paper at a slightly different angle than the one below it. For instance, you could put three pieces of paper angling off to the right and then the fourth one to the left. Flip every 12th piece of paper over so it's upside down.

THE BOOKSHELF

Order the books according to the year of publication or by who gave them to you. When a book has been put back in the wrong spot, you'll know somebody has been mucking about with your books.

SPY LOG 2.017

As I waited for word from The Network, I investigated the strange lump in my trench coat. I emptied out all of the pockets (which takes some time when you've got so many) and found the latest issue of **Mad Scientist Monthly** magazine. Whoever put it there had to know that I had left my trench coat in the dumpster. And there was only one person who could have known that: the henchman who followed me to and from the alley. Was I holding in my hands a secret communiqué from Felicia's inner sanctum? Why would it be given to me? Was it a trick? Was the henchman actually a mole? There had to be a clue in the magazine…

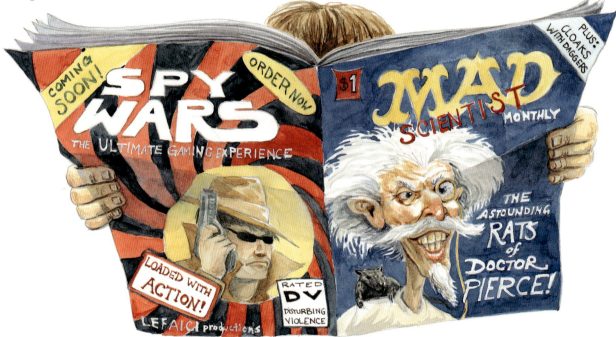

The cover featured a story about a scientist on the verge of a major scientific break-through. Unfortunately, he was about to be kicked out of his lab. Dr. Pierce was performing mind control experiments on rats. He fed them cheese injected with a secret formula, and then showed them videos with subliminal images in them. Apparently, he was trying to get them to dance an all-rat version of Swan Lake. Rats in tutus? Well, I guess you don't get on the cover of **Mad Scientist Monthly** for nothing. No wonder Applegate University didn't want to renew his contract for laboratory space.

Wait. Applegate University? Hmmmmm….

SPY LOG 2.018

The next day, I got a package in the mail. It said, "Do Not Open Until Christmas." Of course, I opened it right away. I carefully unwrapped it and examined the back for secret messages. The present was a framed picture of a very cute kitten. But the picture wasn't important. The **picture frame** was what mattered.

There was a blank piece of paper right where I expected it—sandwiched between the photo and the backing. I held it over a lightbulb, and this is the message that appeared:

HINT: UVORCRZ = FELICIA

OZKGLK MLG SVIV.

UVORCRZ SZH EZMRHVW.

KILXVVW DRGS XAFGRLM.

Yes, Felicia was gone—she was taking no chances. But I had a feeling I was going to hear from the helpful henchman, soon.

PICTURE FRAME MESSAGE HOLDER

Write your message in invisible ink. Then, if anybody looks for a message she'll just find a blank piece of paper.

WHAT YOU NEED
- Picture frame
- Coded message
- Photo*

*Don't use a photo of yourself or your contact. The picture could fall into the wrong hands.

WHAT YOU DO
1. Slide the cardboard backing out of the frame.

2. Sandwich your message between the photograph and the cardboard backing.

3. Replace the cardboard.

4. Carefully wipe your fingerprints off the glass on top of the picture so no one will suspect the presence of a message.

The Cow Caper

SPY LOG 3.001

WEEKS PASSED. Felicia and her henchmen had disappeared completely. Their head-quarters were abandoned. I searched through every newspaper I could get my hands on, desperate for some clue to their whereabouts. Mostly the newspapers were filled with bizarre stories about champion dairy cows disappearing.

I wondered what happened to the helpful henchman who gave me the copy of *Mad Scientist Monthly*. Had Felicia found out he double-crossed her? Had he gotten cold feet?

And what was Felicia going to do with a bunch of video games and a laptop that contained everything you need to know to teach rats to pirouette? There was a connection there somewhere...if only I could find it.

Okay, so I didn't spend ALL of my time thinking about Felicia. I spent a lot of time veg-ging out: playing an awesome video game called *Spy Wars* and eating cheesy junk food. The cheese came from a new company—Lefaici Productions. There was something oddly familiar about that name.

SPY LOG 3.002

One day I received a letter in the mail. I don't have a nephew named Frank in Wisconsin. And I am certainly not Aunt Olivia. None of The Network's contacts were stationed in Wisconsin, so this letter could only come from one person: Felicia's henchman. It must be in  **letter code!**

HINT: READ ONLY THE FIRST TWO WORDS OF EACH SENTENCE.

Dear Aunt Olivia,

We are having a great time. In Wisconsin, there isn't much to do but relax and drink lots of milk. Check out this marvelous state some day.

Lefaici Productions—where I'm working—pays well, and I get a generous vacation package. It's a great time to visit, so pack your bags soon.

Cover for me with mom—she never understands why I keep leaving without saying goodbye. Felicia's plan is to work here for at least six months, and then we'll set up production facilities around the world.

Please come visit. Before it's winter. Too late! It already looks like snow. May be cold soon.

Your Loving Nephew,
Frank

LETTER CODE

This is a great code to use when you think an enemy might see it.

WHAT YOU NEED
- Pen
- Paper

WHAT YOU DO

1. Write a letter to your contact that doesn't say anything relating to your spy work. Construct the letter so that the first two words in each sentence reveal your message.

2. As long as your contact knows to read only the first two words in each sentence, he'll get your message.

3. You can easily create your own letter code. For example, instead of the first two words in each sentence, use the third letter of the second word in each sentence to spell out your message.

SPY LOG 3.003

I had to get to Wisconsin as soon as possible. I dashed off a letter to my contacts at The Network, letting them know about the new developments:

HINT: SRYVPVN = FELICIA

V ARJ FBHEPR FNLF GUNG SRYVPVN VF VA. VZ BA ZL JNL. NTRAG B

I couldn't leave with all my spy things lying around. I was pretty sure that letter came from the henchman, but what if Felicia sent it? It could be a ruse to get me out of my place so Felicia could rifle through my stuff again. I would have to secure my spy files before I left. To hide my real spy information, I made a **fake wall** in the bookcase.

Fake walls are easy to make and always fit into a spy's room décor.

WHAT YOU NEED
- Bookcase with no back
- Measuring tape
- Scissors
- Cardboard
- Old newspapers
- Paintbrush
- Paint that matches the wall
- Glue
- 4 film canisters
- Tape

WHAT YOU DO
1. Take the books off the bottom shelf of the bookcase. With the measuring tape, measure the space between the sides, top, and bottom of the shelf.

2. With the scissors, cut the piece of cardboard to fit.

3. Spread out the newspapers and put the cardboard you cut on top of them.

4. Use the paintbrush to paint the cardboard so that it matches the wall. Let the paint dry.

5. Glue a film canister to each corner of the cardboard. Let the glue dry.

6. Put the fake wall in place. Replace the books. You now have a secret narrow hiding place.

FAKE WALL

54

While I was at it, I figured I'd leave a few fake clues lying around to throw any snoopers off my trail. I pulled out my handy  **book safe** and filled it with fake coded messages and pictures of strangers I had taken during a boring stakeout. Whoever found my book safe would think he had found real information and spend time deciphering the codes and guessing who the people in the pictures were.

Now that my room was secure, I could concentrate on preparations for my trip to Wisconsin.

One of the most famous spy tricks is the book safe.

WHAT YOU NEED

- Hardcover book
- Metal-edged ruler
- Scissors
- Cardboard
- Pencil
- Craft knife
- Small paintbrush
- White glue
- Wax paper

WHAT YOU DO

1. Find a hardcover book you can destroy. Choose one that looks like a book you'd actually read.

2. With a ruler, measure the size of the pages and use scissors to cut a piece of cardboard the same size. Now subtract 1½ inches from the size of the page, and draw a square or rectangle this size in the middle of the cardboard. (This will be the size of the secret compartment.) With a craft knife, cut out the center square to make a template.

3. Open the book to somewhere around page 20 or 30. Place the template on the right-hand page of the book. Line up the edges of the cardboard with the edges of the page. Trace the inside of the template onto the page.

4. Use the ruler and craft knife to cut out the area. Cut a few pages at a time. Don't try to cut too deeply. Remove the cut part of the pages and repeat until you've cut all the pages to the end of the book. (You can leave the last few pages uncut if you like.)

5. Glue all the cut pages together using a small paintbrush.

6. Place the sheet of wax paper between the cut and uncut pages and close the book. Put a heavy weight on top and leave the book to dry overnight.

7. The next day, open the book to the cut and glued pages. Brush a thin coat of glue along the outer edges of the cut pages. Replace the wax paper and let it dry.

SPY LOG 3.004

It was time to put together a disguise. Creating ☁ **the perfect disguise** takes planning and ingenuity, so I spent a few productive hours surfing the internet. (I needed to know what the Wisconsin locals wore.) Before long, my shopping list was ready: overalls and pillows.

Felicia and her henchmen would be watching out for anyone who looked a bit like me. So I decided to ☁ **change my size**—with the pillows.

THE PERFECT DISGUISE

The best place for finding items for your disguise is at a thrift store. There's always something a bit suspicious about walking around in brand-new clothing. Counterspies are always on the lookout for that type of behavior.

When choosing clothing for a disguise, keep a few things in mind:

- Your clothes shouldn't attract attention.
- If it makes sense for your clothes to be dirty, make sure they are.
- Remove all labels from your clothes (if you get caught, your clothes won't give you away).
- If your shoes are too big, wear thick socks. You can stuff cotton balls, or even another sock, in the toes. (You'll trip over your feet at exactly the wrong moment if you don't.)

You can use padding to change the shape of your body, especially if you're worried about being seen by a counterspy or if the disguises you found at the thrift store are a little too big.

WHAT YOU NEED
- Scarves
- String
- Hand towels
- Pillows or cushions

WHAT YOU DO

1. Wind the scarves around your arms and legs (see figures 1 and 2). Use the string to tie them in place.

Figure 1

2. Wrap the towels around your shoulders to make them look broader. Use the string to tie them in place.

3. Use the string to tie the pillows or cushions around your waist (see page 56).

Figure 2

4. Put your disguise on over the padding.

CHANGE YOUR SIZE

SPY LOG 3.005

I was sorry to leave my game station and *Spy Wars* at home, but the situation in Wisconsin sounded urgent. Perhaps I'd discover more clues to the mystery of why a criminal mastermind would want a bunch of video games, a stolen laptop, and a cheese production company called Lefaici.

SPY LOG 3.006

As soon as I got to Wisconsin, I found a phonebook and looked up "Lefaici Productions." With the address and hours of operation in hand, I quickly headed out to find the place.

From a distance, Lefaici Productions looked like any other self-respecting cheese-producing farm, but all my instincts told me there was something far, far more sinister going on. How would Lefaici Productions appear up close?

I spotted two of Felicia's henchmen outside the barn. I quickly constructed an **instant telescope** and zeroed in on one of the cows. Sure enough, it was branded with another farmer's brand. As I snapped a few pictures with my camera, I thought about those newspaper articles I'd been reading. I bet these were the champion cows that had been kidnapped. If I could get this information to The Network, they could at least bust Felicia and her cronies for cow-napping.

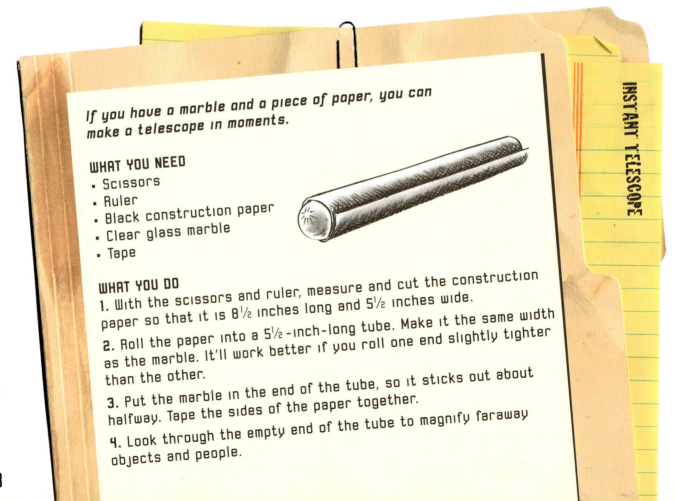

INSTANT TELESCOPE

If you have a marble and a piece of paper, you can make a telescope in moments.

WHAT YOU NEED
- Scissors
- Ruler
- Black construction paper
- Clear glass marble
- Tape

WHAT YOU DO
1. With the scissors and ruler, measure and cut the construction paper so that it is 8½ inches long and 5½ inches wide.
2. Roll the paper into a 5½-inch-long tube. Make it the same width as the marble. It'll work better if you roll one end slightly tighter than the other.
3. Put the marble in the end of the tube, so it sticks out about halfway. Tape the sides of the paper together.
4. Look through the empty end of the tube to magnify faraway objects and people.

SPY LOG 3.007

When I got back to my hotel room, I prepared a message to send to The Network. I printed out copies of the pictures of the cows I had taken, too.

Here's the message I sent to The Network:

HINT: 21-22-15-18-24-18-26 = FELICIA

21-22-15-18-24-18-26 19-26-8 25-22-22-13 16-18-23-13-26-11-11-18-13-20 24-12-4-8. 8-22-13-23 26-20-22-13-7-8 18-13 7-12 26-9-9-22-8-7 19-22-9 18-14-14-22-23-18-26-7-22-15-2. 8-12-14-22-7-17-18-13-20 14-12-9-22 23-26-13-20-22-9-12-6-8 18-8 20-12-15-13-20 12-13.

I built a false-bottom box to send the message and the photos in. If anyone intercepted my package, all he or she would find was a pretty scarf and a birthday card. The Network would know what to do with the box. If all went well, the agents would be here tomorrow morning.

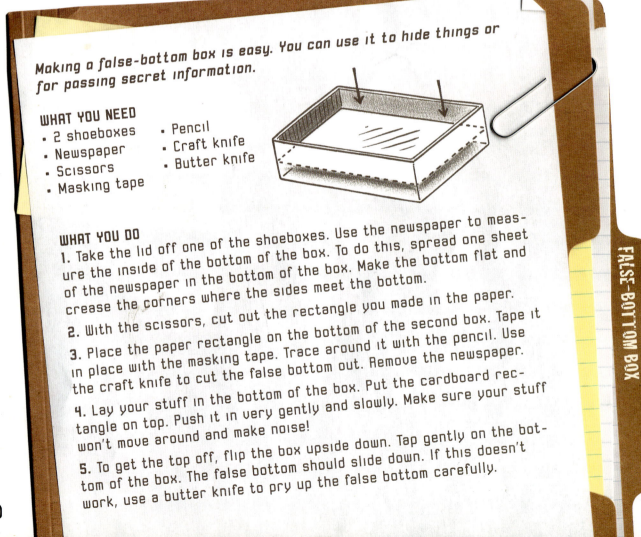

Making a false-bottom box is easy. You can use it to hide things or for passing secret information.

WHAT YOU NEED
- 2 shoeboxes
- Newspaper
- Scissors
- Masking tape
- Pencil
- Craft knife
- Butter knife

WHAT YOU DO
1. Take the lid off one of the shoeboxes. Use the newspaper to measure the inside of the bottom of the box. To do this, spread one sheet of the newspaper in the bottom of the box. Make the bottom flat and crease the corners where the sides meet the bottom.
2. With the scissors, cut out the rectangle you made in the paper.
3. Place the paper rectangle on the bottom of the second box. Tape it in place with the masking tape. Trace around it with the pencil. Use the craft knife to cut the false bottom out. Remove the newspaper.
4. Lay your stuff in the bottom of the box. Put the cardboard rectangle on top. Push it in very gently and slowly. Make sure your stuff won't move around and make noise!
5. To get the top off, flip the box upside down. Tap gently on the bottom of the box. The false bottom should slide down. If this doesn't work, use a butter knife to pry up the false bottom carefully.

SPY LOG 3.008

Sure, Felicia and her henchmen would be in custody within hours, but they would only be brought up on cow-napping charges. I needed to discover the extent of Felicia's plan for world domination so that The Network could put her away for a long time.

I was glad I had remembered to pack my **night-stalking outfit.** I pulled it out and suited up. I was going back to Lefaici Productions.

NIGHT-STALKING OUTFIT

Contrary to popular belief, block isn't the best color to hide in at night. It'll actually draw more attention to you...

WHAT YOU NEED
- Clothes in shades of gray, dark blue, and dark green
- Bandanas or scarves in shades of gray, dark blue, and dark green
- Safety pins

WHAT YOU DO
1. Put on the clothes. The different shades of dark colors will help you blend in with the shadows. Wear old clothes that are smooth and quiet. Make sure you aren't wearing clothes that leaves and brush will cling to.

2. Tie bandanas and scarves around your arms, legs, or waist. This will help break up your outline, so you won't be so noticeably human-shaped.

3. Tuck or pin any loose bits of cloth to yourself. You don't want to trip over them or have them sna on things.

I got back to the farm at dusk. There was a lot of ground to cover if I was going to get close enough to see anything. And unfortunately, there wasn't a lot to hide me from view. I would have to 🐾 **crawl** through the grass.

Crawling well is a lot harder than it looks. Fortunately, I'm an expert so I could devote part of my brain to thinking about what Felicia was up to...

Here are three different kinds of crawling methods. The one you use on your mission will depend on how high the cover is.

THE CAT CRAWL

This one is good for crawling behind low walls and through waist-high vegetation. Get on your hands and knees. Keep your back flat. Lift your hands and knees just far enough to clear the ground. Don't drag your shins along the ground—you'll make noise and leave an obvious trail. Hold your head still.

CRAWLI

THE FLAT CAT CRAWL

If the plants around you come up to your knees, you'll have to get a little lower. Lie on your stomach. Shift your weight to your left side. Stick your left arm straight out in front of your head and bend your right knee. Put your right hand close to your shoulder. Keep your elbow close to your body. Shift your weight onto the right side of your body, lifting the left side very slightly and moving forward. Flatten out, then bend your left knee and do it again. Be careful not to drag your body along the ground too much. You'll make lots of noise and leave a path for an enemy agent to find.

THE BELLYACHE

This is as low as you can go. You will flatten all of the plants you crawl over, so this won't help you escape from an enemy agent who's tracking you. Lie on your stomach. Put your arms out in front of you, flat on the ground. Put your legs out behind you. Turn your feet so your arches are touching the ground. Pull yourself forward using your hands and feet. Don't break contact with the ground.

ASSIGNMENTS FROM THE SPY ACADEMY

Night-Stalking Skills

Gather some friends and a flashlight. Find a park or field with several different kinds of cover. (Check out your backyard–it may be perfect for this game.) Pick one person to be the first guard. She gets the flashlight. Everyone else lines up on one side of the playing space and tries to sneak to the other side without getting caught. The first person to make it to the other side without getting caught becomes the next guard. When the guard thinks she sees or hears somebody, she turns the flashlight on that spot and yells, "Freeze!" If she catches somebody in the flashlight beam, he has to go back to the starting place. If nobody is there, she gets two more tries to capture someone. If she misses three times, the person closest to her becomes the guard.

SPY LOG 3.010

I crawled up to the barn window and peered inside.

Felicia brought out the latest line of sample cheeses from Lefaici Productions, and the henchmen immediately devoured them. I noticed that Felicia didn't eat any of the cheese. After the eating was done, she opened the stolen laptop and pushed a button. An ear-splitting siren blared throughout the barn.

The henchmen scrambled to the other side of the room, out of my sight. When they came back, they were all wearing tutus!

As Felicia pushed buttons on the laptop, the henchmen lined up in front of her. Slowly, they began to dance. Sort of. It was like they were in a trance or something. They were all trying to do the same thing, but whatever they did, it wasn't what Felicia wanted them to do. The more frustrated she got, the faster she pushed buttons on the laptop, and the henchmen whirled around faster and faster. The deafening siren continued.

In some weird way, I felt like dancing too. My arms started to raise over my head like a ballerina, and I had a sudden urge to wear a tutu! What was wrong with me? I plugged my ears to block out the incessant siren sound the laptop was making.

Immediately, I no longer felt like dancing. And it was at that moment that I realized Felicia's plan for world domination. Could it be true? The stolen dairy cows, the cheese, the *Spy Wars* video, and the stolen laptop? It all made sense now. I must contact The Network!

As I jumped up, I stumbled over a hay bale and bumped into a large milk can. The milk splashed all over me as the can banged to the ground. Felicia looked toward the window. Had she seen me? She started shouting at the tutu-wearing henchmen, "Get that spy!" I ran across the field as fast as I could, leaving a trail of milk. I could only hope to make it to my hotel before the henchmen could catch up with me.

SPY LOG 3.011

I raced into the hotel, passed a perplexed concierge, and locked the door to my room. I threw my milk-covered costume in the shower. (I had to destroy all evidence that might place me anywhere near the Lefaici Productions barn.)

I needed to get a message to The Network fast. This was the perfect time to use The Network's emergency email account. Agents are instructed to use it only in dire straits. Since the lives (or at least the minds) of the agents sent to arrest Felicia were at stake, I figured this counted.

I quickly coded this message on my computer:

HINT: ◗◼□◻✱◼✳ MEANS WARNING

◗◼□✱◼✳ ◻□□□◻✱✳ ▼✱✳ ◗□◻ ◗✱□✎
✱◼✳ ✱◻□□◆✱✳▲ ✱□ ◻▼ ✱✳ ◗□
✱✱✱▲✳ ✱□◻ ◻✱✳✱✳ □□□◆▼✱□▲
✱ ✱✱▲□◆✱□ ✱✱◻✱✳ □□▼ ✱□
◗□◻ ✱□◻✱◼▼✱□ ▲✱✳ ▲◻□□✱ □✱
▼✱ ✱✱✱▲✳ ▼□ ▼✱✳ ◻✱◻□□▼□□ ✱□
▼✱▼✱◼✳ ✱✱▼ □✱ □□ ▼✱ □✱✱▼ □✱ ✱▼
▲✱ □◆▼ □□ □✱◻□✱✱ ◻✱◻✱ ✱◻▼□□◻
✱□□◆□◻✳ ✱◼ ▼✱ ✱✱✱▲✳ ◗◆▼✱ ▲□◗ ◗□◻▲
✱□□ ▲◆□◻✱□✱◼◻◻ ✱◻✱✱✱✳ ✱✱▲▼□□◻ ◻◻◻
✱□□✱✱✳ □✱ ▲□ ◗□◻▲ ✱◻◻✱✱✳ ◗▲ ✱□✱◼✳ ▼□
◆✱✳ ▼✱◻◻ ▼□ ◻◻✱✳ ✓✱◻□◻◻◼✳ ✱◼ ▼✱ ◗□□◻
□✱◗ ✱✱□

I pressed SEND and waited. (I kept the door locked, though.) Five hours later, I received this reply in my inbox:

HINT: ⌑⚬⌇⌂⚏⌸⚎ⱳⱶⱶⱵⱸⱱ⚏⚬⌇⚏
IS CONGRATULATIONS

⌑⚬⌇⌂⚏⌸⚎ⱳⱶⱶⱵⱸⱱ⚏⚬⌇⚏
⌸⌂Ⱶ⌇⚎ ⚏ ⚏ⱳⱸ ⌸⌂Ⱶ⌇⚎⌸
⚏Ⱶ⚎⚏ⱱⱵⱵⱵ⚎ ⚎∞Ⱶ
⌑⚬⌊⚏ ⚎∞Ⱶ ⌑∞ⱵⱵⱵ⚏Ⱶ
⌸⌇ⱱ ⚎∞Ⱶ ⱶ⌸ⱶⱶ⚏⚬ⱶⱶ ⌇⚬⌊
⚎∞Ⱶⱸⱱ ⌸⚏Ⱶ ⱱⱵⱵ⚏⚏⚎ ⚬⚏
ⱱⱵⱶⱸⱱ ⌊⌸⌂⚏Ⱶ ⚎∞Ⱶ
⌂⌸⚒ⱵⱵ ⌑⚬⌇⚏⌸⌂ⱱ⌇ⱱ
⚏ⱳⱶⱶⱵ⚏⚒ⱱ⌇⌸ⱶ
⌇⚒⌸⌂ⱵⱵ ⚬⚏ ⱶⱶⱵ⚬ⱶⱶⱶⱵ
ⱶ⚎Ⱶ⌸⚏⌇⚏ ⱱⱵⱶ⚬⚏ⱱ⚬ⱶ
ⱶ⌸⌊⚏ ⚎⌸⌑ⱱⱱⱶⱱ⚬⚎
ⱱⱵⱶⱸⱱ ⌑⚬⚒ⱶⱶⱳⱵ⚏Ⱶ
⚏⚬ⱵⱵⱵ⚏⚒ⱱ ⌸⌇⚏ ⌑ⱵⱱⱵ
⌸Ⱶⱱⱱⱸⱱ ∞⌸⌊⚒⚏⌑ ⌸⌊⌊
⚏ⱶ ∞Ⱶⱱ ∞Ⱶⱶⱑ∞∞⚒Ⱶⱶ
⌸ⱵⱱⱵ ⱱⱱ ⌑⌸⌊⌊Ⱶⱱⱸⱱ
ⱱⱱⱵⱸⱱ ⌊ⱳⱵⱱ ⌊ⱶⱱ ⱑ⚒Ⱶⱶⱸⱱ
⌑⌸ⱱⱵⱵⱱⱶⱳⱶ⌊ ⱶⱵⱶ⌊ⱱ
⌑ⱱ⌸ ⚒Ⱶ⚏⌑⌸ⱶⱶⱱ⚎ ⱶ∞Ⱶ
ⱶ⌇⚬⌸⚏Ⱶ ⚬ⱱ⚬ⱳ ⚏ⱱⱵⱱ⚎
Ⱶ∞Ⱶ ⚬⌇Ⱶ ⚏∞⚬
ⱱⱸⱵⱱ⌊ⱸⱱ ∞ⱱⱵ ⱶⱶ⌸ⱸⱸⱱⱵ
⌸⌊⚏ ⚒⌸⚬⚏ ⱶ⚒ⱵⱵⱸ
⌂ⱸⱵⱑⱸⱵⱶ⚎

The Network didn't need to worry about me. I still had plenty of clever disguises that Felicia hadn't seen. I could always make myself **look older.**

OLD EYES
It's easy to make your eyes look older than they really are.

WHAT YOU NEED
- Mirror
- Soft dark eyeliner pencil

WHAT YOU DO
1. In front of the mirror, crinkle up one of your eyes so that you can see the wrinkles at the edge.
2. Trace over the wrinkles with the eyeliner pencil.
3. Repeat steps 1 and 2 on the other eye. (If you don't, you'll look pretty suspicious.)

Often, your eyes are all you need to change to make yourself look older. If you want to go all-out, you can make your mouth look older, too.

OLD MOUTH
Making your lips look older is a good technique to combine with old eyes.

WHAT YOU NEED
- Make-up that matches your face
- Lipstick
- Soft, dark eyeliner pencil

WHAT YOU DO
1. Rub the foundation on your lips to make them paler.
2. Draw new lips with the lipstick. Make them slightly thinner than your real lips.
3. Make thin lines around your lips with the eyeliner pencil. These will look like wrinkles.
4. Pull the corners of your mouth down, like you're frowning. Draw dark lines where you see the creases.

If you do go this far, make sure that you're wearing a disguise that incorporates gloves and a scarf or turtleneck. If you don't cover your hands and neck, they'll draw attention to you because they'll look a lot younger than your face.

SPY LOG 3.012

Felicia's plan for world domination had been foiled.
The Network closed down Lefaici Productions, and
even though it was impossible to retrieve every
copy of *Spy Wars*, The Network was able to destroy
every remaining package of formula-tainted cheese.
When I returned to my home, I threw away my *Spy
Wars* video game.

   Everything was slowly returning to normal (well,
as normal as a spy's life could get). But, with
Felicia on the loose, The Network was worried
that I was in danger. They even told me to
disappear for a while. But I wasn't worried.
Like all good spies, I still had a few tricks up
my sleeve.

**FELICIA AND I WILL MEET AGAIN. SHE WILL NOT
GET AWAY NEXT TIME. IF YOU HAPPEN TO FIND HER
FIRST, YOU NOW KNOW WHAT TO DO.**

— Agent O

68

ASSIGNMENTS FROM THE SPY ACADEMY

Mission: Disappear
Location: Wherever you are
Tools: None
Accomplices: None

- Always take a different route between two points.
- Never take the shortest route.
- Pay for everything in cash.
- Make a list of all the places you usually go. Never go to any of those places again.

Dear Reader,

   We, the publishers, have been granted special permission to print selected pages from Agent O's actual Super Secret Spy Notebook. The Network, working through a team of government lawyers, decided the following pages would provide a good sense of Agent O's methods and techniques without compromising national security. Our own team of lawyers (okay, a friend of a friend whose friend is a lawyer) is fighting to someday publish Agent O's uncensored Notebook. Stay tuned! We haven't heard from Agent O since receiving this book. Agent O's whereabouts are currently unknown.

DO YOU HAVE WHAT IT TAKES TO BE A SPY?

- Razor-sharp wits
- Amazing powers of perception
- Patience
- Perseverance
- Curiosity

RULES TO SPY BY:

- Don't get caught.
- Use your powers for good. Only bad guys spy for personal gain.
- Deflect attention from yourself.
- Wear sunglasses whenever you can.
- Never take the most direct route.
- Watch for hidden cameras and alarms.
- Keep a pen and a rubber band in your pocket at all times.
- Always have an alternate route.
- Keep your trench coat handy.
- Never reveal the identity of a fellow spy.
- Write everything in code (especially your journal!).
- Plan ahead of time.
- Always have at least two alternate plans.
- Never underestimate your enemy.
- Don't let anybody take your picture.
- Make your own spying gadgets and disguises.

Class: ALERT YOURSELF ALARMS

Lecture: #278

Topic: THE HAIR ALARM

No matter how top-secret your secret agent status is, sooner or later somebody is going to come snooping. The best defense is to know when you've had an intruder.

WHAT YOU NEED

Door or drawer

Piece of hair

WHAT YOU DO

1. Pull a piece of hair out of your head.

2. Lick it, and stick it across the door and the doorframe. (Make sure you don't have to open the door again.) Put it up high if you're tall, or down really low if you're not. Make sure it's at a height that your enemy can't see.

3. If you're working with a drawer, put the piece of hair across the drawer and the frame.

4. If you return and the hair is gone, someone opened the door, while you were out.

Class: ALERT YOURSELF ALARMS

Lecture: #499

Topic: THE DRAWER TRAP

If you have a desk drawer where you keep secret stuff, you can put an alarm it.

WHAT YOU NEED

Drawer

Piece of tape

WHAT YOU DO

1. Open the drawer below the one you want to put the alarm on.
2. Tear off a small piece of tape about 1½ inches long.
3. Stick one end of the tape to the bottom of the drawer you're putting the alarm on. Stick the other end to the casing.
4. If anyone opens the drawer, the end of the tape on the casing will detach and stick to the bottom of the drawer.
5. To check whether the drawer has been opened, open the drawer below and look up at the bottom of the drawer you put the alarm on.

(If you open the drawer you put the tape on before checking it from beneath, you won't be able to tell whether you set off the alarm or somebody else did.)

Class: ALERT YOURSELF ALARMS

Lecture: #278

Topic: THE BOOK TRAP

This technique will let you know if someone's been snooping in your top-secret journal.

WHAT YOU NEED

Piece of hair

Book

Good memory

WHAT YOU DO

1. Place a piece of hair on a specific page of the book. Place it so that it could easily fall out if anybody flipped through the book. Practice a few times to get the placement of the hair perfect.

2. Remember which page you put the hair on. Even if your enemy spy is observant enough to notice there was a hair in the book, he won't be able to put it back exactly where you had it.

OTHER IDEAS

—Leave copies of fake top-secret journals lying around to see whether enemy spies are snooping. Book trap each journal, so if someone does snoop, you'll know that all they discovered was false information.

Class: CUNNING CODES

Lecture #: 2314

Topic: INVENTING CODES

Always write messages in code. When inventing a code, make sure your contact knows what the code is (duh!). There are countless variations of every code you can imagine.

WHAT YOU NEED
Pencil

Piece of paper

WHAT YOU DO
1. Write all the letters of the alphabet going down the left side of the paper. If you'd like to be able to use numbers in your code, add them at the bottom of the list.
2. On the right side of the paper, write a different letter, number, or symbol across from each letter in the alphabet. This is called a cipher.
3. Memorize your code. Use the cipher to write a message. Then, dispose of the cipher.

Class: CUNNING CODES

Lecture #19

Topic: DISPOSING OF SECRET MESSAGES AND CIPHERS

Once you've deciphered a secret message or invented a code, get rid of the evidence. If an enemy spy found these notes, she'd have no trouble decoding your secret messages.

METHOD	PROS	CONS
Shredding	Good for the environment. You can snoop through the recycling bin while you do it.	It takes time. Paper cuts. A truly zealous enemy spy could put the message back together.
Burning	No one can reconstruct a document that's been turned to ash.	A fire in your spy hideout is hardly inconspicuous. Not to be done by under-aged spies without adult supervision.
Eating	No one will ever read it. Health experts claim fiber is good for you.	Paper doesn't taste very good.

Class: CUNNING CODES

Lecture: #395

Topic: THE POCKET PROTECTOR CODE

This code is great for secret meetings.

WHAT YOU NEED

Pocket protector

Different colored pens or pencils

Shirt with a breast pocket

The Simple Code

WHAT YOU DO

1. Make each color of pen or pencil represent one code item.

For example:

Red	Danger
Yellow	Message waiting
Blue	No message
Green	All clear
Purple	Come back later
Black	Code is broken

2. Put the pen or pencil that says what you need it to in the pocket protector. For instance, you create a code that says "Danger, come back later" by putting a red and purple pen in your pocket.

3. Carry all the pens or pencils in a different pocket. That way, you can update the message whenever you need to.

The Complex Code

WHAT YOU DO

1. If you have more complicated things to communicate, start by making each space on the pocket protector represent a different thing.

For example:

First hole	Status (i.e., danger, all clear, code broken)
Second hole	Time
Third hole	Place
Fourth hole	What

2. Now assign a different meaning to each color for every space in the pocket protector. For instance, the blue pencil might mean "all clear" if it's in the first hole and "after lunch" if it's in the second hole.

For example:

Red: Danger; sunset; the office; message

Blue: Meet me later; after lunch; the bathroom; dead drop

Green: Follow me; after school; the cafeteria; rendezvous

Yellow: The code is broken; before school; the auditorium; eavesdrop

3. Rearrange your pens or pencils as needed.

— Make sure you and your contact are following the same code!

— It is particularly important that you agree whether the code will be read from left to right from the perspective of the person seeing the code or wearing it. If you don't make sure, all your communications could be backward.

Class: CUNNING CODES

Lecture: #77

Topic: INSTANT MESSAGES

Spies can make messages from just about anything. Here
are some quick message ideas:

— If you know it's going to rain, you can make a signpost
out of pebbles. Some examples:

message waiting

keep going

go the opposite direction

stuck to the top of the mailbox

— Or you can use a piece of string. Tie knots in it to
indicate the message. Some examples:

go home

check the bushes

watch out for the spy

under the flowerpot

— You can stick the piece of string between cracks in a fence or tie it around a branch. Make sure your contact knows where to look for the string.

— Use a leaf. Manipulate it in various ways—for instance:
- Tear a corner off the leaf
- Tear the stem off the leaf
- Tuck the stem through the front or back of the leaf (each can mean a different thing)

— Arrange the CDs or books on your shelf in a certain order.

— Rest your pencil in different places on your desk. (Front left corner, back right corner, top middle, bottom middle, etc.)

Class: CUNNING CODES

Lecture: # 97

Topic: INSTANT INVISIBLE INK

There are all sorts of ways to make invisible ink. It's possible to make invisible ink out of the supplies in your desk—if you brought an apple for lunch!

WHAT YOU NEED

Apple or lemon

Sharp pointy tool (a paper clip or toothpick works well)

Paper

WHAT YOU DO

1. Stick the sharp pointy tool into the flesh of the fruit.
2. Cover the tip of the tool with juice.
3. Write your secret message on the paper, using the tool as a pencil.
4. When you need more ink, repeat steps 1 and 2. Do this until you've written the entire message.
5. Let the message dry.

To read the message:

- Hold it over the top of a lightbulb and turn on the light.
- Put it in an oven at 300°F. (If you put the paper on a cookie sheet first, it'll be easier to take out of the oven.)

Class: CUNNING CODES

LECTURE: # 429

Topic: PUNCH CODE

Spies love using newspapers to hide their messages. This code
is a classic.

WHAT YOU NEED

Newspaper

Piece of cardboard

Code

Pin

WHAT YOU DO

1. Place a page of the newspaper on top of the cardboard.

2. Find the first letter of your code at the beginning of one of the
articles on the page.

3. Use the pin to prick a hole in the letter.

4. Find the next letter you need for your code and prick a hole in
that one.

5. Continue to prick holes in each letter until you've written your entire
code. Make sure that you prick the letters in order—otherwise you'll
confuse your contact.

6. Hold the letter or newspaper article up to the light to find the
letters to the code.

Class: DEVIOUS DISGUISES

Lecture: #334

Topic: SUCCESSFUL DISGUISES

One of the key components to any good spy repertoire is the ability to disguise oneself successfully. You don't need fancy disguises! In fact, the most successful disguises have more to do with how you move your body than what you wear.

WHAT TO DO

1. Spend time watching people.
   — Pay attention to how different people stand, sit, move their heads, use their hands, and more.
   — Keep a list of all the different ways people move.
   — Imitate them.

2. Practice these techniques when nobody's watching:
   — Walk with your toes pointed toward each other.
   — Walk with your toes pointed away from each other.
   — Take long, quick strides. Stand up straight and swing your arms.
   — Take short, slow steps. Put your hands in your pockets and shuffle your feet.
   — Limp. Don't forget which side you're favoring!

3. Since spies often dress up like repairmen and waiters, observe real repairmen and waiters.
   — Figure out how they move when they're performing specific aspects of their job (such as checking meters or carrying a tray of dishes) and the order in which they do things.
   — Someone who is pretending won't be able to imitate them perfectly. (If you can imitate them perfectly, no one will be able to figure out you're really a spy.)
   — Knowing how people behave will help you spot enemy spies pretending to be repairmen and waiters.

4. Other techniques:
   — Avoid being photographed. You don't want anybody to have a record of what you look like or where you've been. Sneezing fits will often take you out of the camera's viewfinder.
   — Keep in the shadows at night. Don't step into bright lights.
   — Carry a quick disguise with you. Reversible coats work particularly well, as do hats and sunglasses. You can put them on quickly and then look like a whole different person.

Class: DEVIOUS DISGUISES

Lecture: #132

Topic: THE TELEPHONE

The telephone is an important spy tool. Keep these things in mind.

1. Don't let your call get traced. Ways to avoid this:
    — Fancy equipment
    — Use a pay phone
    — Use a phone in a public place (library, restaurant, coffee shop)
    — Borrow a cell phone from unsuspecting passer-by.
2. Be careful of background noise. Use it to confuse your enemy rather than letting her know where you are.
3. Disguise your voice.
    — Fake accents are not the best way to disguise your voice.
    — If there are people watching, purse your lips like you're about to start whistling. Then raise or lower your voice. Don't let it waver while you're speaking. (Practice in the shower.)
4. If no one can see you, use any of the following methods to disguise your voice:
    — Muffle the receiver with a hat, handkerchief, glove, or scarf.
    — Hold your nose.
    — Put a pencil between your teeth.

Class: DEVIOUS DISGUISES

Lecture: #99

Topic: CHECKING FOR FAKE DISGUISES

It's important for a spy to know when a person isn't what she appears to be. Here are some ways to check suspicious-looking people for fake disguises.

1. Face makeup: Pretend there's dirt or food on the suspect's face and offer to wipe it off with a handkerchief. The person will back away suspiciously to avoid having his cover blown.
2. Fake beard: Pretend there's a bug stuck in the beard and offer to get it out. Yank a bit on the beard. If the person doesn't yelp, it's fake.
3. Fake hair: Perform the fake beard test, but on the suspect's hair (obviously).

Note: Be very careful about running into dogs you know while in disguise. You smell the same to a dog, no matter what you're wearing or how you're moving.

Class: DEAD DROPS

Lecture: #24

Topic: TWIGGY MESSAGE DISGUISE

A stick is a good way to hide a message, especially if you want a sturdy hiding place.

WHAT YOU NEED
Stick, at least as thick around as your thumb

Screwdriver

Sandpaper (optional)

Piece of paper

WHAT YOU DO
1. Find a decaying stick with a soft middle.
2. Break the ends off the stick. You can make it any length you want, but it should be at least short enough to hide in your pocket easily.
3. Use the screwdriver to make a hole through the middle of the stick.
4. If you'd like, roll a thin strip of sandpaper into a tube and rub it around inside the stick. This will make the hole bigger and smoother.
5. Cut a strip of paper narrower than the stick is long. Write the secret message on the paper, roll it into a tube, and put it in the stick.

Class: DEAD DROPS

Lecture: #69

Topic: DISGUSTING DISGUISES FOR MESSAGES

When you make covers for your secret messages, you'll decrease the chances of anybody accidentally finding them—particularly if the cover is really disgusting.

WHAT YOU NEED

Hollow plastic dog poop from a novelty or joke store

Craft knife

Secret message

WHAT YOU DO

1. Flip the dog poop over.
2. Make a 3-inch slit in the back of the dog poop with the craft knife.
3. Stick the secret message inside.
4. Put the dog poop in the dead drop spot.

Class: DEAD DROPS

Lecture: #456

Topic: PICTURE-PERFECT HIDING PLACE: PART I

You can stash messages underneath posters on your locker, flyers in the hallway, or anything else that hangs on a wall. This technique is perfect for metal lockers, refrigerators, or anywhere else that a magnet will stick to.

WHAT YOU NEED

Glue	Heavy books
Picture or small poster that fits inside your locker	Thin, self-adhesive magnetic strips
Cardboard	Envelope
Wax paper	Locker or other metal surface

WHAT YOU DO

1. Glue the poster to the cardboard. Put the wax paper on top. Stack the heavy books on top and let the glue dry.

2. Flip the poster over. Stick the magnets along the edges of the cardboard, at least 1/4 inch in from the edges. Position the magnets before removing the adhesive.

3. Glue the front side of the envelope to the center of the cardboard.

4. Put the poster in your locker. Stash secret messages in the envelope on the back.

Class: DEAD DROPS

Lecture: #456A

Topic: PICTURE-PERFECT HIDING PLACE: PART II

If you're in a hurry, use this quick-and-dirty method instead.

WHAT YOU NEED

Poster

Tape

Mirror (optional)

WHAT YOU DO

1. Tape the top edge of the poster to the locker.

2. Flip the poster up and tape secret messages onto the locker. Flip the poster back down to hide the messages.

3. Make sure you aren't being watched when you use this hiding place. If you'd like, hang a mirror in your locker. You can pretend to be checking your hair when you're really looking around for enemy spies.

COOL SPY WORDS

CIPHER: changing words in order to hide what they mean

CODE: see cipher

COMMUNIQUÉ: a message

CONTACT: the person with whom a secret agent exchanges information

DEAD DROP: a place where you leave information for your contact

DECODE: to translate a coded message

DECOY: a fake message or body-double intended to fool your enemy

DISGUISE: clothing that helps you look unlike yourself, or like someone else

DOUBLE-CROSS: when an agent switches sides

ESPIONAGE: a big word for spying

HEADQUARTERS: the gathering place for agents

HENCHMAN: someone who helps a criminal mastermind

INTERCEPT: to get a message intended for someone else

INVISIBLE INK: ink that disappears as you write with it

MESSAGE: information passed between two agents

MOLE: an agent who's working for the enemy

MORSE CODE: a method of communicating

MULTIPLE-AGENT TAIL: more than one agent using teamwork to follow a suspect

PERISCOPE: a gadget that uses mirrors to let you see around things

PROTOCOL: the rules a spy organization follows

RECON: short for reconnaissance, it means gathering information about a place or person

RENDEZVOUS: a meeting between two spies

SECRET AGENT: someone who gathers information and saves the world from evildoers

SIGNPOST: a signal that lets your contact know there's a message waiting

STAKEOUT: keeping a close watch on a place

SUSPECT: someone you believe has committed a crime or is part of your enemies spy ring

SURVEILLANCE: keeping a close watch over someone or something

TAIL: following someone closely to find out more information

CIPHERS

Code giving you trouble? Try using these ciphers to decode it.

MORSE CODE PAGE 32		CIPHER PAGE 56	CIPHER PAGE 51	CIPHER PAGE 60	CIPHER PAGE 66	CIPHER PAGE 67
.-	= a	N = a	Z = a	26 = a	✳ = a	▯ = a
-...	= b	O = b	Y = b	25 = b	✸ = b	∪ = b
-.-.	= c	P = c	X = c	24 = c	✳ = c	▣ = c
-..	= d	Q = d	W = d	23 = d	❄ = d	† = d
.	= e	R = e	V = e	22 = e	✳ = e	✕ = e
..-.	= f	S = f	U = f	21 = f	❋ = f	⌿ = f
--.	= g	T = g	T = g	20 = g	✳ = g	▣ = g
....	= h	U = h	S = h	19 = h	✳ = h	∞ = h
..	= i	V = i	R = i	18 = i	✳ = i	⤴ = i
.---	= j	W = j	Q = j	17 = j	✳ = j	∅ = j
-.-	= k	X = k	P = k	16 = k	✳ = k	— = k
.-..	= l	Y = l	O = l	15 = l	● = l	⊔ = l
--	= m	Z = m	N = m	14 = m	○ = m	※ = m
-.	= n	A = n	M = n	13 = n	■ = n	♭ = n
---	= o	B = o	L = o	12 = o	▢ = o	2/10 = o
.--.	= p	C = p	K = p	11 = p	◰ = p	‖ = p
--.-	= q	D = q	J = q	10 = q	◱ = q	▣ = q
.-.	= r	E = r	I = r	9 = r	◲ = r	⚅ = r
...	= s	F = s	H = s	8 = s	▲ = s	▦ = s
-	= t	G = t	G = t	7 = t	▼ = t	▣ = t
..-	= u	H = u	F = u	6 = u	◆ = u	∿∿ = u
...-	= v	I = v	E = v	5 = v	❖ = v	⚓ = v
.--	= w	J = w	D = w	4 = w	◗ = w	λ = w
-..-	= x	K = x	C = x	3 = x		= x	◇◇ = x
-.--	= y	L = y	B = y	2 = y	▮ = y	⊙▣ = y
--..	= z	M = z	A = z	1 = z	▮ = z	⚇ = z

THE CODES: DECODED

Use these answers to check your decoding skills.

RUBBER BAND MESSAGE (PAGE 11)

Follow the woman in the blue coat.

INVISIBLE INK (PAGE 16)

The hideout is on the north side of town. I'm coming back tomorrow with a periscope to figure out if she has the games.

SIGNPOSTS (PAGE 20)

— message waiting

= no message

✗ drop ruined

〰 next to the creek

〰〰 in the tree

WET PENCIL WRITING (PAGE 25)

Send in a sneaky agent to retrieve the one video game with the info on it. Enclosed are the photos of the hideout from my recon mission. Leave the rest of the video games there. I want to figure out what this woman is up to. Send me any info you have on her.

SODA CAN COVER-UP (PAGE 27)

The game has been retrieved. Spies around the world have files on the woman. Her name is Felicia. She's a criminal mastermind. Keep an eye on her.

CROSSWORD CLUES (PAGE 28)

Felicia's henchmen stole a laptop from Applegate University Lab. Find out why.

FLASHLIGHT SIGNALS (PAGE 32)

We will bring the laptop to the back room of the Candy Shack at two.

IN THE FILE (PAGE 33)
Just kidding!

WAX PENCIL MESSAGE (PAGE 42)
Felicia does not have it. I'm being watched. Mission aborted.

INVISIBLE INK (PAGE 43)
The laptop is being taken to the airport. You should be able to retrieve it from the third locker on the left anytime after lunch.

PICTURE FRAME MESSAGE HOLDER (PAGE 51)
Laptop not here. Felicia has vanished. Proceed with caution.

LETTER CODE (PAGE 53)
We are in Wisconsin. Check out Lefaici Productions. It's a cover for Felicia's plan. Please come before it's too late. It already may be.

SUBSTITUTION CODE (PAGE 56)
A new source says that Felicia is in Wisconsin. I'm on my way. Agent O

NUMBER CODE (PAGE 60)
Felicia has been kidnapping cows. Send agents in to arrest her immediately. Something more dangerous is going on.

COMPUTER SCREEN CODE (PAGE 66)
warning approach the barn wearing earplugs do not eat any cheese from lefaici productions i discovered felicias plot for world domination send samples of the cheese to the laboratory for testing get rid of the rest of it she put dr pierces mind control formula in the cheese watch spy wars for subliminal images destroy all copies of spy wars felicia was going to use them to make everyone in the world obey her

EMAIL REPLY CODE (PAGE 67)
congratulations agent o our agents retrieved the cows the cheese and the laptop now they are destroy ing the copies of spy wars the games contained subliminal images of people breaking into banks hacking into computer systems and creating havoc all of her henchmen are in captivity but be very careful feli cia escaped she knows you were the one who foiled her plans and may seek revenge

ACKNOWLEDGMENTS

Thanks to everyone who helped make this book, especially:

Jason Chin, whose illustrations and sense of humor brought this book alive; **Celia Naranjo,** for her astute reading, brilliant visualization, and constant enthusiasm; **Nicole Tuggle,** the inspiration for the Fabulously Felonious Felicia (you may not be nearly as evil, but you fake it well!); **Chelsea Pryor Wise** and **Chance Barry,** kid code breakers extraordinaire, who tested and suggested many of the codes in this book.

This book wouldn't have been possible without the help of **Joe Rhatigan, Nathalie Mornu, Orrin Lundgren,** and **Karen Levy.**

Thanks for the moral support from **Deborah Morgenthal, Steve Livingston,** and my **parents.**

And special thanks to **Veronika Alice Gunter, Delores Gosnell, Jonathon Stansell, Suzanna Roettger,** and **Ben Reid.** They kept me sane, fed me, contributed wacky ideas, read early drafts, and patiently accepted lots of rain checks.

INDEX